WHISKEY STRAIGHT WOMEN
literary biographies

Virginia Aronson

ISBN: 978-93-6354-537-3

First Edition: 2025
Rs. 200/-

Cyberwit.net
HIG 45 Kaushambi Kunj, Kalindipuram
Allahabad - 211011 (U.P.) India
http://www.cyberwit.net
E-mail: info@cyberwit.net

Printed at Repro.

CONTENTS

INTRODUCTION

The five women writers depicted in this collection led lives soaked in whiskey and ink. Each woman was a limited edition writer, brilliant and uniquely talented, able to make a name for herself in fiction or poetry, short stories or novels. These women lived through the sexism of their time and managed to achieve success while struggling to balance a career with a home life. Some were more successful at this than others.

As writers, the women in this collection were indentured servants to their work, some to their families as well. As creative individuals growing up and living in different parts of the world, they saw things differently, which gave them each a distinctive voice. They were able to share their views in their writing, impacting the culture while challenging social expectations for women in the 20th century—and beyond.

All of these writers were heavy drinkers. The whiskey (and wine and gin and…) did not grant them artistic vision but may have provided some relief from the stress of financial, social, gender, and time constraints. They resorted to drinking in order to numb pain and relieve sadness, but alcohol typically served to deepen their troubles instead.

The history of literature has been chronicled by male writers. Yet women writers throughout history have established a public voice, using the power this provided to speak out for change. To write with authority entails projecting extreme confidence. A writer has to maintain cynicism and emotional detachment, achieve a selfish hoarding of time and energy, and remain separate in order to observe, analyze, create, and share. This can be much more difficult for women, especially when they have a family. Such challenges are heroic, yet familiar to us all.

In a published review of her first book of poems, **Dorothy Parker** was praised as being "whiskey straight." Famous for her sharp, often funny observations about society, she also wrote poetry that warned women to regard love with the skeptical eye it so often deserved. She inspired women to share their pain and their wit. But she struggled with writer's block, poverty, loneliness, and alcoholism until the end of her life.

A Creole from a small Caribbean island, **Jean Rhys** was sent to school in England. For the rest of her life, she remained an outsider while her heart belonged to Dominica. Her early writing illustrated a woman's difficulties balancing an independent spirit with financial dependence on men, but her most successful novel came late in life: *Wide Sargasso Sea* told the story of a fictional young woman from the tropics who goes mad after she is married off to a man from England. Rhys' own life was one of poverty, failed affairs and marriages, and heavy drinking. She believed a woman could trust only herself and her writing.

French novelist **Marguerite Duras** had the courage to publish her personal experiences as a woman who opened herself to alcohol, sex, freedom, and solitude. She promoted the truth of women's writing as a means of access to political reality, awareness, and change. Writing and love affairs were her ways of returning to a primitive state she considered to be both existential and essential. Her films were avant-garde, strange, and, for her, exciting explorations of a new realm of art. Alcohol was, by her own admission, the only lover she was faithful to for her whole life.

American Gothic horror writer **Shirley Jackson** juggled the responsibilities of a suburban American wife and mother with her massive success as a writer. Her short story "The Lottery" is one of the most widely read and discussed works of American 20th century fiction and a cultural touchstone. Her fiction addressed the mythic sense that society must work to keep in check powerful forces of great destruction. In her own life, she felt controlled by men—financially, professionally, and sexually. She used her inner darkness to recreate the feeling of domestic horror, exploring the exploitation and desperate isolation of American wives. By employing terror, hauntings, and the uncanny in her work, she cleverly exposed some of the real challenges for women of her era: the social pressures, the distrust, and the lack of money, time, and personal space. Pressure on women not to challenge the happy housewife role society was forcing upon them created the tension that animated her writing. Her own home life became increasingly unhappy, and she developed agoraphobia while attempting to leave her unfaithful and belittling husband. Overweight and a heavy drinker, she died in her sleep before turning 50.

A difficult and talented woman, **Patricia Highsmith** entranced people, leaving behind a legacy of broken hearts and bestselling books. She led a closeted life masking a fear of discovery while enjoying much success with her novels. Her first book was adapted to film by Alfred Hitchcock, and more popular movies came later including *The Talented Mr. Ripley* and *Carol*. She used her writing to illustrate the annihilation of the self and the potential for rebirth as someone else. Her stories often had homoerotic overtones. She chose to live in Europe, where she drank heavily in her later years and lost popularity due to her abusive, racist rants.

***

The poems that follow create a kind of speculative literary biography for each of these important writers. All of these poems are meant to highlight the bravery and power of a handful of women who dared, despite the odds and the challenges, to write whiskey straight.

1. DOROTHY PARKER
(1893-1967)

Dorothy Parker on Dorothy Parker

I wrote, said, was known for
my vinegar wit
my tart one-liners
my sardonic sophistication
speaking, writing my mind
competing with men
flaunting my sex
a role model for women
in the flapper 1920s
the way I tossed off men
love, death, so acerbic
but inside fluttered
a wounded baby bird.

The night I was born
at our summer house
on the New Jersey shore
a hurricane ripped off
the chimney, and oh
what an entrance I made
to my New York family
the Upper West Side
well-to-do socialites
steeped in money, loss
I watched my mother
die young, stepmother
when I was 9 and later
my uncle on the Titanic.

What fresh hell is this?

I left Catholic school
I left boarding school
to take care of my father
until he died, oh death
followed me like a dog
little orphan Dottie
no money left, left
alone in the Big Apple
a petite plain brunette
big-eyed pixie in green
a cloche hat
a wiseacre mouth.

I can't tell you when
exactly
I began to drink more
alone, Scotch
without water or ice
murdering the highballs
living in a haze
a dreamlike peace
a whiskey mist.

No matter how successful
I still felt insecure
a fragile bird
flightless, afraid
singing when unhappy
oh, what a goddam song!

Dorothy Parker on Her Heart

A plucky feisty flapper
fresh faced and razor sharp
but inside I was hiding
a sorrowful heart
always waiting
for some damned man!

I married the first one
in the rush of the war
a handsome officer
introduced me to gin
returned to me ruined
a morphine addict, drunk
scratch a lover, I said
you'll find a foe
we parted then
I put all my eggs
into one bastard
had an abortion
reached for the bottle
tranquilizers too.

Three more times
I felt solidarity
with the voluntary dead
scars on both wrists
wrapped in black velvet
ribbon and bows
and once I drank
a bottle of shoe polish
but lived to tell it
as a wry joke.

Men seldom make passes
At girls who wear glasses

Alone in my old age
cash did not sully
these bony fingers
and death came slowly
then, typically, suddenly
my poor battered heart
chipped like my headstone
that said Pardon My Dust
after so many decades
my ashes forgotten
in a file cabinet
in a lawyer's office
while they waited
for some damn man
to bury me right!

Her First Husband
(Edwin Pond Parker II)

When I met her she was small
a woman you could woo
breathe her woody scent
run hands down slim hips
have lively discussions
her sweet gentle voice
sharing words of love.

Time sharpened her edges
her soft speech peppered
with bricklayer swears
her radical views
cutting bitch wit
deep sense of injustice
anger at the rich which
I took personally, insulted
as provider in our home
scion of a fine family
successful stockbroker
she seemed to reject all
that she had come from
that I was giving her
she bit the open hand
of her master once
too many times.

After the war
I returned from the front
different than I'd left her
alone for two years
I was not a fit

with her artsy crowd
except our shared thirst
little short drinks
all through the day
and out all night

'til I left her
for my mother
in the dry suburbs
of upscale Connecticut.

The Algonquin Round Table (1919-1929)

You can lead a horticulture
but you can't make her think.

So quick with the wit
she wrote little poems
satirizing rich matrons
their banalities, bigotries
and *Vogue* published her
and hired her
an editorial assistant
then staff writer
at *Vanity Fair*
a magazine, she said
of no opinions
while she had plenty

a tough critic
a real New York wag
like one of the boys
at the big round table
at the Algonquin Hotel
in the speakeasy days.

Brevity is the soul of lingerie.

The word got around
about the wonks at the Gonk
in the Rose Room for hours
their antics soon fodder
for newspaper columnists

all the hangers-on
all woozy afternoon.

She lived on the second floor
came downstairs
to raise hell every day
nothing else mattered
but jazz clubs and brothels
Haig & Haig and bathtub
gin under the table
all of us floating
on a sea of booze.

A hangover is the wrath of grapes.

Her Second Husband
(Alan Campbell)

I was a Broadway actor
handsome but underutilized
when she swept into my life
her incandescent humor
her firebrand charm
and I convinced her
to love me despite
my undesirable desires
we moved to L.A.
where *the streets were paved*
with Goldwyn she said
we could write scripts
with roles for me.

We went straight
to the top and lived
in Beverly Hills
a pretty house
a yard full of dogs
romping and writing
screenplay after screenplay
her scorn for me
growing daily.

I escaped to the Air Force
officer training school, Miami
swimming pools and barracks
good friends, a better life
overseas
I met a woman
and did not return.

Her Third Husband
(Alan Campbell)

Between writing gigs
she got dumped in Mexico
by yet another playboy
crawling back to me
we wed again
a bouquet of big smiles
for the moment
for the newspapers
in the California sunshine
rapidly fading to shadows
drinking, bickering
until she fled
to New York, always
back to New York.

She moved to a modest
residential hotel
dark halls full of shuffling
lonely elderly women
gray widows, spinsters
in soft slippers, housecoats
afraid to die manless
she wrote a play
about them, herself
a success on the stage
a traveling show.

The only thing to expect
from Dorothy Parker
was the unexpected.

2. JEAN RHYS
(1890-1979)

Jean Rhys on Jean Rhys' Life

I was born an island
on a Caribbean isle
plantation descendant
Ella Gwendolyn Rees Williams
Gwen they called me
white cockroach, scuttling
away from cruel voices

I buried myself in books
my father a doctor, drinker
my mother with a whip
her fat family estate
built on sugar slavery
gone after emancipation
but she never understood
how much they hated us

I spoke with a lilt
patois of my birthplace
so I couldn't be an actress
when they sent me to England
16 in the midnight street
thirsty for sunshine, sea air
in the chill blue of London
drab, joyless, fogbound.

City life a new dream
pale crowds in gray light
all around me men
like flabby fish
lording over a small tank
and staring out

with glassy eyes
I only wanted night
to lie on the bed and
pull the past over me
like a warm blanket
to hear time slide past
a river running, running.

The men who loved me
supported me financially
did not care
I was young
I had to go on
living and living and living
a chorus girl, a mistress
posing nude
for artists in Paris
in seedy European clubs.

I wrote from this place
I wrote about myself, scared
I'd be a mournful dog
without a master

all those grim years
the dim fire kept alive
all the rooms, rooms
a place for me to hide
from the wolves outside.

Jean Rhys on Jean Rhys' Loves

I married three times, two
went to prison, one
kind, devoted, true
but my heart hardened
to cement after breaking
on the backbone of my first
lover a wealthy stockbroker
spotted me onstage
at 19 a virgin and he
called me kitten unaware
the rooming house stairs
smelled of cat piss
he wooed my poverty
unaware it was the cause
of compromises with him.

Desperate and hungry
I took him on
I fell for him
I was kept
in furs and finery
before I was dumped
like back alley garbage
and I wrote
from that empty place
filling up notebooks
with vivid intense lives
poor women on their own
limited by their bodies
by men, for men
I was ahead they said
of my time…

I saw it differently.

I married handsome Jean
our firstborn died
and later another
our baby daughter
spent years in homes
Jean in prison for theft
while I waited for him
above the pub
drinking and writing
as Jean, Jean Rhys.

Leslie my editor
promoter, protector
a good husband
until his death
then his cousin
Max replaced him
a happy man, naive
convicted of fraud
jailed and again
I was left
alone

in my own little cell
I disappeared
my books out of print
the few who cared
thought me dead
while I was struggling
troubles inflicted
and self-inflicted
writing out by hand

my masterpiece:
Wide Sargasso Sea.

Whiskey in one hand
champagne in the other
a visit with the Queen
little island girl
at the masked ball
without a mask
Creole Gwen
white cockroach.

Her Secretary
(David Plante)

When you tell the story
make it funny she said
her mumbled words
smooshed and stirred
in the wrinkled mouth
in the sweet vermouth
in the gin she had me add
to the ice she claimed
the hotel would not provide
the hotel of old people
in pink, in armchairs
in a daze she cried
told me her tears
were 92% booze.

She blamed fate
England, men, and me
some days
I wanted to throw
her memoir off a bridge
let the river take it
let the drinks flow by
when she laughed, I smiled
when she wept, I looked sad
but her moods changed so fast
sometimes I grinned
while she cried and tears
came to my eyes too
when she said her work
fed a giant lake all writers
must contribute to big rivers

and small streams she told me
to dip in my bucket, go deep.

Rain hissed in a tin sky
and when she fell in
the toilet
that time I forgot
to re-lower the seat
she called out
for me
and I fished her out
all bones and tremble
I kissed her
damp forehead
the sweat smell
of gin, aging, fear

she was afraid
of people
she told me, but not
trees, woods, the wild
animal roar
of perpetual waves
of the crashing sea
and I was afraid of her
and what I wanted
from her
for myself.

3. MARGUERITE DURAS (1914-1996)

Marguerite Duras on Her Childhood

My parents were teachers
working in Indochina
my father went home
to Duras, France
to his hometown
to die.

Bereft, Mother moved us
around the Mekong Delta
lagoons, deltas, creeks
a bungalow by the sea
on land we built up
dikes, embankments
mud and log walls, debt
to the white colonial scum
who lied about our property
how the sea rushed in
swamping the crops
depleting our savings
killing our happiness.

We moved to Saigon
Mother headmistress
at the native school
on cobblestone streets
lit by flickering gas lamps
lined by tall palms
tamarinds, flame trees
in the French quarter
sweet smell of jasmine
lingering in warm air

Mother like an old crone
in her widow's black.

My older brother
stole, gambled, smoked
in opium dens, pimped
made Mother beat me
and love him more.

My other brother
handsome, simple
my dear friend
immersed in nature together
hunting the swamps
for parrots, snakes
hiking the forests
full of chattering monkeys
escaping the wrath at home
I slept with him
and then at 14
an older man
a scandalous lover

my mother said well,
men like her for
who she is and
that's how she is.

Her North China Lover

Shocking that she wrote
about her first love
affair with a tall, pale
handsome Chinese
man in a raw silk suit
black limo, blue house
on the way
to her boarding school
crossing the Mekong
to early adulthood.

He gave her a ride
he was 27 and she
an untamed schoolgirl
he the educated scion
of a banking fortune
a millionaire delinquent
with lots of mistresses
and a child in her
in his bachelor quarters
in the Chinese district
of bustling Saigon.

All this is untrue
her first lover
a native
Vietnamese
small, coarse
so ugly he repulsed
stalked, threatened her
she resisted, a child
with long auburn braids

skinny and flat chested
her mother desperate
for money she made
her daughter the bargain.

Indochina was all empty sky
rice paddies far as one could see
poor peoples' faces, bent bodies
rickety huts and dirty children
bony yellow dogs, ribbed ox
carts on straight white roads
through endless green fields
under a veiled sun, wet earth
in the monsoon darkness
she saw so much there
so much nothing.

All this is true
the ludicrous mismatch
he paid off their debt then
his father paid her mother
to take her away
her white skin so thin
it shimmered on moonlit sheets.

Even then she had a taste
for weak boys, men
who cried and softened
so she could love
them hard, leave them
shocked, he said
she would always
move on from love

and she did
that is true.

Her Secret Lover

Afternoons in hotel rooms
unknown to their partners
his wife, three kids
her child and two men
they worked well together
behind her back though
he had many others
she never saw
through the façade
of good looks, charm
and lies, his secret forte.

She guided his first book
into print, still superior
his rage emerging, merging
over whiskey
Campari, beer, fists
brawling like lovers can.

Apart for weeks
she went off alone
writing, writing
detoxing from drinking
until she finally discovered
what everyone else knew.

He thought her dangerous
a witch, a curse
he was only 43
too young
for the Don Juan death
in a seedy hotel.

She had a strange power
he thought with her
he could destroy death
with writing, love
drinking he thought
they'd killed death.

And she said: *You think
love is something
we make up?*

Her Last Love
(Yann Andréa)

An alcoholic, trashed
broken down body, wasted
the years they were in love
not lovers, he preferred men
four decades younger
he was 28, a grad student
and she was drunk
when he called her up
one of the many fans
in the cult of Duras
the tension between people
alcoholism and eroticism
the French youth mad
for her, a drug
he couldn't live without.

That first time he called
they talked and talked and
she said he should come visit
he slept in her son's room
for the next sixteen years
in the old hotel by the sea
in her big house in the country
and he never left
her side unless carousing
the clubs and casinos
she gave him free rein
despite her intense jealousy
of his sex life with men.

She was always writing
drunk, drinking
red wine by the case
whiskey from a flask
late into the night
always returning
to the distant exotic
land of her childhood
trying to understand
her lingering fear
her abject loneliness.

He took care of her
while she wrote
book after book
on the inner shadow
the secret archives
of her most secret self.

4. SHIRLEY JACKSON
(1916-1965)

Shirley Jackson on Shirley Jackson

Houses were in my blood
my great-greats built San Francisco
mansions for the robber barons
Victorians for the rest of us
raised in tight lipped families
rejecting others' otherness
disapproving always
when I married a Jew
bohemian intellectual writer
an outsider like me.

Stanley thought I was great
a master of Gothic horror
I thought him untrustworthy
sleeping with all the coeds
at the little red whorehouse
on the hill
his campus
his fat-faced tomatoes
at the Vermont college
up the street from the house
I bought with my royalties
after "The Lottery"
made my name.

But I became stuck
afraid to stay
afraid to leave
subsumed into a husband
four children, our house
that lonely island
in a sea of ruin

backdrop to the small
domestic incidents
writ large
beginning and ending
with a house
always a house
the only place
in those days where
a woman had control.

My houses were settings
for the helter-skelter lifestyle
for our psychological states
our passions and regrets
a hope chest for dreams
the lure of the devil
that lurks in our minds.

Shirley Jackson on Witchcraft

The constant strain to be
someone other than myself
a troubled struggle between
what I wanted
and what was expected of me

from a young age I was too
fat, sloppy, smart, uninterested
in what was socially acceptable
my mother belittling me
I had so little self-
confidence, so much shame
about my looks, my habits
kicked out of college
for skipping class.

In my childhood bedroom
hunched over my desk
I heard voices
a kind of devil visit
a kind of mythic rite
a kind of passage
from the world
of rejection
to a place
of understanding

and I began to write
about fear, fear
about the problems
that defined women's lives
when behavior fails to conform

when refusing to play the role
leads to tragic psychic results.

After I married Stanley
I became a faculty wife:
formal dress, styled hair
entertaining academics
at the perfect dining table
crisp white napkins
clean matching china
clean matching china
drinking, drinking
me so drunk
guests so polite

but with poison
beneath the pose.

Her Widower
(Stanley Edgar Hyman)

She liked to toss bombs
stand back, watch them
EXPLODE
and he didn't know
she had one ready
after twenty-five years
making his coffee
his meals, the diet food
his doc ordered, drinking
canned slim shakes with him
driving him in her Morris Minor
laughing at his drollery
and overlooking, getting over
his many slip-ups, sins

and they were getting along
they were good that afternoon
she went upstairs to nap
after a pleasant summer
lecturing, traveling
to read her work
her voice dour, direct
projecting the doom
beloved by her fans

and busy writing
a new novel
in a different voice
a widow on a trip
to a new city
a new name

a new life
unencumbered
by husband
children
homemaking:
no HOUSE
no haunting
responsibilities.

And when he finally
went upstairs
to wake her:
BOOM
she was gone.

5. PATRICIA HIGHSMITH
(1921-1995)

Patricia Highsmith on Her Influences

She tried to abort me
drinking turpentine before
I was born he'd left us both
and it changed me
poisoning my life

as Mary Patricia Plangman
always a disappointment
didn't appreciate, didn't conform
displeasing, distrusting
my mother and my stepdad
a grey-black spirit of doom

dragging me away
from my home in big sky Texas
to the gritty streets of New York
lost and scared they sent me
back to Grandma in Fort Worth

I never knew why or when or if
they would come for me
and I hated them

when I joined them in Manhattan
belonging no place, not there
not Queens, Greenwich Village
I chose Barnard, literature
stylish clothing, affected poses
drinking my way up the ladder
with society girls and gin
whiskey shots in bars
women and booze and writing

about identity and deception
the fears and furies of secret selves
the subterfuge of the repressed

Graham Green calling me
the poet of apprehension
my characters got the revenge
I wanted for myself.

Patricia Highsmith on Her Sexuality

My first was for a man
writing scripts for comics
freelancing and living alone
dead broke in Taxco
the Mexicans knew how
to drink cheap all day

I headed to Yaddo
writer's colony in the woods
met the man I would not marry
promised him and hurt him
completing my first novel
for a British publisher
and Alfred Hitchcock
adapted it for the screen

I was headed for top rungs
while suffering from cycles
of anorexia and alcoholism
therapy helped me understand
the psychology of the psychopath
and I felt I understood
I was a man
who loved women
and mistreated them

seducing the straights
breaking up couples
the two Pats
the charmer, the offender
battling inside, on the page
my life a novel I made up

lies in interviews
in my diaries fantasies
inventing until the end

I left millions to Yaddo
my literary estate to the Swiss
my heart in a bottle
of whiskey and turpentine.

Her Writer Lover
(Marijane Meaker)

They met cute
in a lesbian bar
in the 1950s
they could be arrested
for the love they made
MJ taken with her
gentlemanly manners, good
bones and thick dark hair
her laughter, shared
book talk and gay gossip
MJ wanted to *be* her
Pat
a literary lion
a lesbian icon.

Isn't it wiser to accept
that life has no meaning
is what she said
the earth like the moon
with only her on it
her dark fantasies
keeping her going
all those years
all those books
stories of men who compete
who climb, who con, who kill
for the thrill in her novels
about the American Abroad
an excuse for excess
self-indulgence, hedonism
how she lived herself

from villages in France
to villages in Greece
Venice and Positano.

The two writers
settled down together
in an artsy community
in the Pennsylvania countryside
fruit trees and Pat gardened
cooked and dressed
for dinner, formal
slacks, a crisp white shirt
bright ascot, polished loafers
with a shiny switchblade
from her blazer pocket
she trimmed indoor plants
and sipped her second martini
while studying the dictionary—
a strange cocktail hour

Pat affectionate, easygoing
didn't want her mind
cluttered up with bad feelings
didn't hold grudges
or believe in analyzing
herself or her characters
she preferred to leave
the unconscious mind.

Perhaps I don't like anybody
was how she explained
her characters' lack
of decency, humanity
her own prejudices

her own shifting identity
her withdrawal, escapes
from love affairs
like theirs

while above her a window
filled with light blue sky
just out of her reach
too small
too far away
to escape through.

REFERENCES

Dorothy Parker:
Marion Meade, *Dorothy Parker: What Fresh Hell Is This?* Penguin, 1989.
Gill Paul, *The Manhattan Girls: A Novel of Dorothy Parker and Her Friends*, Morrow, 2022.
Michelle Dean, *Sharp: The Women Who Made an Art of Having an Opinion,* Grove Press, 2018.

Jean Rhys:
Caryl Phillips, *A View of the Empire at Sunset*, Farrar, Straus and Giroux, 2018.
David Plante, *Difficult Women: A Memoir of Three,* New York Review Books, 1983.
Miranda Seymour, *I Used to Live Here Once: The Haunted Life of Jean Rhys*, W.W. Norton, 2022.
Polly Teale, *After Mrs. Rochester,* Nick Hern Books, 2003.

Marguerite Duras:
Alain Vircondelet, *Duras: A Biography,* Dalkey Archive Press, 1994.
Laure Adler, *Marguerite Duras: A Life*, University of Chicago Press, 2000.

Shirley Jackson:
Ruth Franklin, *Shirley Jackson: A Rather Haunted Life*, W.W. Norton, 2016.
Shirley Jackson, *Life Among the Savages*, Farrar, Straus, and Young, 1953.
Shirley Jackson, *Raising Demons*, Farrar, Straus, and Cudahy, 1957.

Patricia Highsmith:

Richard Bradford, *Devils, Lusts and Strange Desires: The Life of Patricia Highsmith*, Bloomsbury, 2021.
Anna Von Planta, Editor, *Patricia Highsmith: Her Diaries and Notebooks 1941-1995*, Liveright/Norton, 2021.
Marijane Meaker, *Highsmith: A Romance of the 1950s*, Cleis Press, 2003.

SUGGGESTED READING

Fiction and Poetry by Dorothy Parker:
The Portable Dorothy Parker (2006)

Fiction by Jean Rhys:
Quartet (1929)
After Leaving Mr. MacKenzie (1931)
Voyage in the Dark (1934)
Good Morning, Midnight (1939)
Wide Sargasso Sea (1966)

Memoir by Jean Rhys:
Smile Please: An Unfinished Biography (1979)

Fiction by Marguerite Duras:
The Impudent Ones (1943)
The Easy Life (1944)
The Lover (1984)
The North China Lover (1991)

Fiction by Shirley Jackson:
"The Lottery" (1948)
The Birds' Nest (1954)
The Haunting of Hill House (1956)
We Have Always Lived in the Castle (1962)

Nonfiction by Shirley Jackson:
The Witchcraft of Salem Village (1956)

Fiction by Patricia Highsmith:
Strangers on a Train (1950)
The Blunderer (1954)

The Talented Mr. Ripley (1965)
Carol (1990; originally published in 1952 as The Price of Salt)

ACKNOWLEDGMENTS

Poems were published or accepted for publication in the following literary journals with altered titles and in shortened form, some under another (pen) name:

Synchronized Chaos: "The Algonquin Round Table," "Patricia Highsmith on Her Influences," "Patricia Highsmith on Her Sexuality," "Her Writer Lover"

Misfit Magazine: "Dorothy Parker on Her Heart," "Shirley Jackson on Shirley Jackson," "Shirley Jackson on Witchcraft," "Her Widower"

Fictional Café: Dorothy Parker: "Her First Husband," "Her Second Husband," "Her Third Husband"

Dear O Deer!: Marguerite Duras: "Her Secret Lover"

ABOUT THE AUTHOR

Virginia Aronson is a poet, novelist, and textbook writer who lives in the lush, lurid tropics. Her poetry collections include *Farmlandia,* a novel in verse from Cyberwit. Her chapbooks include *Hikikomori, Itako,* and *Tropical Diagnoses.* Her work has appeared in many literary journals and has been nominated for multiple awards.

www.ingramcontent.com/pod-product-compliance
Ingram Content Group UK Ltd.
Pitfield, Milton Keynes, MK11 3LW, UK
UKHW040038200726
13845UKWH00054B/468

9 789363 545373